# TH
# BIG B

For Georgia — R.R.

# THE BIG BANG

Written by

## RICHARD ROBINSON AND JONATHAN SANDERSON

Illustrated by

## RICHARD ROBINSON

Published in association with
Yorkshire Television

**h**

Hodder
Children's
Books

a division of Hodder Headline plc

The Big Bang production team:
Mark Bridge
Diane Chapman
Rosemary Cleary
John Francas
Anna Kost
Colin Nobbs
Jonathan Sanderson
Patrick Titley
David Pitt
Gabrielle Bradshaw

Published by Hodder Children's Books 1998

10 9 8 7 6 5 4 3 2 1

ISBN 0 340 72711 X

Printed by

Hodder Children's Books
A Division of Hodder Headline plc
338 Euston Road
London NW1 3BH

# INTRODUCTION

Gareth, Kate and Violet are looking forward to guiding you through all these games, gadgets and fascinating facts from The Big Bang TV series. (And they've got some useful tips for you on pages 95 and 96.)

## BIG BANGS AND BRIGHT SPARKS

Here are four things that changed the way we live:

a

b

c

d

Here are the bright sparks who invented them; can you guess who invented what? (Answers at the end of next page.)

A) Percy Shaw was fascinated by the way his car headlights made the eyes of his cat shine back at him through the darkness. He invented...?

B) Thomas Edison knew that passing electricity through a carbon wire caused it to glow white hot. It was a short step from there to his creation of the first...?

C) Michael Faraday saw that a compass needle was deflected by an electric wire. He looked further and found that lots of wires made the compass needle deflect further. If the electric current rotated, so did the needle. He had invented...?

D) William Fox Talbot noticed how silver ornaments go black when exposed to light. He wondered if there was a way to use this effect. By playing around with silver compounds he invented...?

Enjoy playing with the strange and wonderful experiments, games and puzzles in THE BIG BANG BOOK.

Play around enough and one day you will invent something amazing yourself.

Answers:
A) Percy Shaw invented the "Cat's Eye" road reflector (c).
B) Thomas Edison invented the electric light bulb (b).
C) Michael Faraday invented the electric motor (a).
D) William Fox Talbot invented the photographic film and camera (d).

# CONTENTS

# HOT 'N' COLD

**A touch of your fingers makes a glass of water boil!**

## YOU WILL NEED

Tall glass, preferably straight
  sided half-pint
Handkerchief or piece of
  cloth
Elastic band
Water

Fill the glass with water and lay the handkerchief over the top.

Poke the handkerchief into the glass. Fasten the edges over the rim with the elastic band. What happens when you turn the glass over? (DO THIS OVER A BOWL!)

The water that passed through the handkerchief when you poked it into the glass pours away, but the water on the inside stays there! You would expect it to pour through the cloth, or at least weigh it down, but instead the cloth is sucked *upwards* into the glass, forming a beautiful curve.

Two things account for this: The water cannot leave the glass unless something comes along to replace it. Normally that would be air rushing in as the water rushes out, but...

...the air is unable to get through the holes in the handkerchief. Water has a thin "skin" at its surface, and this is surprisingly strong over small distances, such as the gap between the threads of the handkerchief.

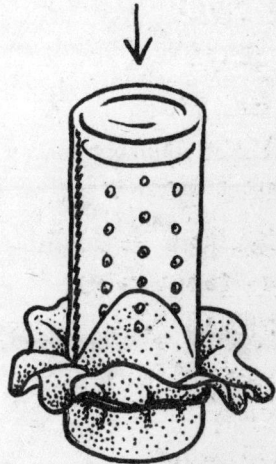

Now hold the glass around the elastic band at the bottom and push down steadily on the top of the glass with your other hand. The water will appear to boil; bubbles will stream up through it.

You are pushing the glass down against the handkerchief, so it is pulled out of the glass. This forces air in through the cloth, and it looks as if you can make water boil with your fingers!

9

# THE SOLID LIQUID

**Don't blame the school cook for the awful custard!
Sometimes it's a liquid, sometimes a solid.**

Custard powder or cornflour
Water
Bowl

Mix three parts custard powder
to two parts water, in a bowl.

Stir it gently and you have a
liquid; but stick your hand
right into it, haul it out of
the bowl and treat it roughly,
and it will go solid. Stop
mistreating it for
an instant, and
it'll turn back
to a liquid.

What you start with is a bowl of
water with the custard particles
floating in it – it behaves like a
liquid. But when you rough-
handle it the water molecules
are knocked into the middle of
the cornflour granules, and get
trapped among them, so the
custard is unable to flow
– it turns solid.

"SHOULD HAVE KEPT
RUNNING..."

# ONE CAN CAN FLOAT ONE CAN CAN'T

## YOU WILL NEED

Two cans of drink, one diet,
  one ordinary (with sugar)
Bowl of warm water
Salt

Put both the cans in the warm water. They will sink.

Now begin to add the salt, stirring to dissolve it properly.

Both the cans have the same amount of drink inside, yet one of them will rise to the surface before the other. Can you guess which one? Can you guess why?

The juices, flavourings, colourings and sweeteners dissolved in the drinks make them thicker, or denser, than water, so that they sink.

Adding salt makes the warm water gradually denser, until it is about the same density as the drinks. Soon both cans will float. But...

The difference between them lies in the sweeteners. Sugar is denser than artificial sweetener, so the less dense diet drink is the first to rise.

# BOOMERANG

BOOMERANG

**Here's a lightweight boomerang for throwing indoors –
if you're careful!**

## YOU WILL NEED

Polystyrene ceiling tile
Pencil and paper
Cutting knife

Gareth's four-winged boomerang
turns in smaller circles than the
traditional two-winged variety,
so it's simple to make it fly
indoors.

Start with a pack of square
polystyrene ceiling tiles from a
DIY shop. Many tiles have grobbly
patterns on them, but try to
find the smoothest ones you
can.

Use the pattern on the opposite
page as described. Get a grown-
up to help you cut out the shape
from the tile, using a sharp knife.
(It'll have to be sharp, or the
polystyrene will crumble.)

To make the booerang come
back, you'll have to bend the
wings up very gently, so it's
slightly dished. Then hold it
vertically, with the bottom of the
dishing away from you. Throw it
straight out, at about the

level of your head. It's more
important that it spins than
that it moves fast, so flick your
wrist as you let go. Getting the
throw right can be a bit tricky,
but keep trying, changing just
one thing about your throw each
time to see what difference it
makes. Are you throwing the
boomerang upwards, when it
should go straight out? Or
tilting it outwards, rather than
holding it vertically? Or throwing
it too hard? Or not spinning it
enough? Keep trying – if Gareth
can manage it, anyone can!

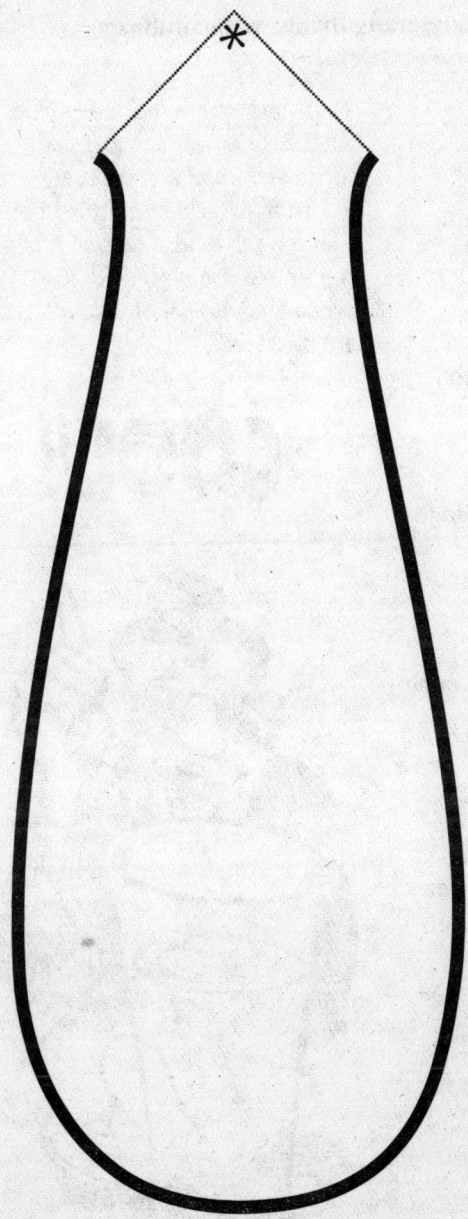

How to draw out your boomerang:

Trace this shape onto a piece of paper, then cut it out.

Place it on the ceiling tile and draw round the thick line.

Turn the shape 90°, keeping the ✽ in the same spot. Draw round the shape onto the tile again. Do this twice more, so that the boomerang shape has four wings.

# COLOUR CHANGE ICE CUBES

**How to improve your party drinks with a cabbage.**

## YOU WILL NEED

Red cabbage
Chopping board and knife
Hot water
Ice cube tray

Don't worry — these ice cubes are made from cabbage water, but they won't ruin your drinks — quite the opposite.

**1** Chop half the red cabbage into small pieces. Place in a bowl and cover with hot water. Leave for a couple of minutes.

**2** Strain the mixture through a sieve to get rid of the bits, leaving you with a blue liquid. Allow this to cool.

**3** Pour the liquid into the ice cube tray and leave in the freezer overnight.

When they are put in drinks, the blue ice cubes change the colours of the drinks in different ways — water turns blue, as you'd expect, but lemonade goes pink, and orange juice goes red.

"Red" cabbage is normally blue, but contains a chemical that turns red when it meets an acid. The fruit juice in the drinks contain a weak acid, and some of the drinks are also coloured, hence the variety of colours that are created.

## COOL!!

# MIGHTY ICE

Ice is easily shattered. Toilet paper isn't exactly strong either.
So what do you think you get if you combine them?
Cold wet toilet paper? Wrong! Extra strong ice!

## YOU WILL NEED

A plastic dish, such as an old
  margarine tub
Toilet paper
Water

**1** Cut the toilet paper down
to more or less fit into the tub –
lots of sheets. (Make sure you
leave enough behind in the toilet,
or someone will be stranded
later on!)

**2** Lay the paper in the tub,
then pour in enough water to
cover it and place the tub in the
freezer.

Laminating, as this layering
system is called, is a common
way to make things strong.
Plywood, fibreglass, paper mache,
etc all get their strength this
way.

When you turn the ice
out of the tub, the ice
will have amazing
strength. Just try
to break it!

# SPAGHETTI TOWERS

**Many things that seem weak and flimsy become surprisingly strong if used in the right way. Try building a tower with spaghetti.**

## YOU WILL NEED

Spaghetti
Marshmallows – small ones
  from the cake-making
  section of a supermarket,
  or large ones cut into four

Use the marshmallows to hold
the spaghetti ends and build a
tower.

To begin with make simple
shapes to see which is
strongest – you'll find that
cubes are wobbly...

...pyramids with square bases
are better...

...but triangular pyramids are the
sturdiest of all.

Have a go. You might be able to
build a tower 40–50 cm high!

Why not have a competition to
see who can build the tallest
tower?

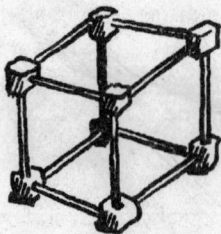

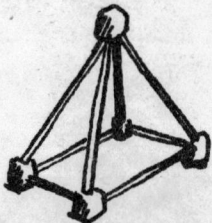

HELPFUL HINTS:

Remember that the spaghetti is good at bearing loads when it's upright, but weak on its side.

Whenever you can, add extra diagonal struts to brace the structure.

Using lots of spaghetti might make the tower stronger, but it also makes it heavier, so however sturdy you make it at the base, keep the upper parts light.

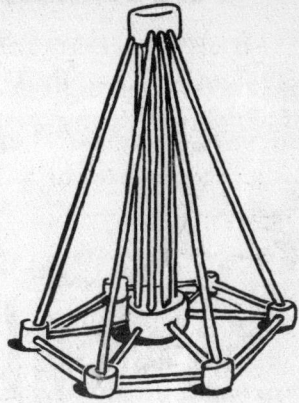

Try building a central column of several pieces, propped up all around with single pieces.

And finally, remember:

DON"T DO THIS IN THE RAIN!

WHEN YOU'VE FINISHED WITH THE SPAGHETTI...

# STRANGE BUT TRUE

## JOSEPH PRIESTLEY, THE MAN WHO PUT THE FIZZ INTO FIZZY DRINKS

Priestley was born in Yorkshire 150 years ago. He was a serious fellow. In fact he became a vicar (hardly surprising with a name like that).

He was for ever asking himself BIG questions, and one of the biggest in his day was "WHAT'S THE WORLD MADE OF?" Nobody knew about atoms, molecules, chemical reactions, elements... most people said that it was all God's work, and to ask too many questions about God was to be nosey on a quite cosmic scale. Priestley got into a lot of trouble for his questions: his house was ransacked, his books were burnt, in the end he had to leave the country, but still the questions nagged him.

One of his obsessions was to find out what air was made of. "Nothing of any importance!" said his fellows. "You can't see it, smell it, hear it or touch it – there's obviously nothing to be bothered about. Stop asking questions. Sssssh!!" And yet, he thought, we should not ignore this vapour just because we can't see it.

Priestley did a series of clever experiments on the invisible gas, air. Before long he discovered that it wasn't one invisible gas he was dealing with, but a whole tribe of them. He "revealed" to the world oxygen, ammonia, nitrous oxide, sulphur dioxide, and carbon monoxide... But the gas that we most remember him for is the one that goes "Sssssssh!"

In the local brewery Priestley saw vats of fermenting beer. The vats were bubbling – giving off an invisible gas. He found that if he put a candle in the gas, the flame was snuffed out. He did more experiments, and discovered that animals couldn't survive in it either. Gradually he pieced together a "profile" of what we now call carbon dioxide.

Quite by accident, he found that if you bubble carbon dioxide through water, it makes it rather nice and fizzy. His new zingy water was called "carbonated water". Nowadays, it is the main ingredient of all fizzy drinks

So when you next buy a bottle of cola, drink a toast to that rather serious vicar who gave us a rather snappy drink.

"...DONT SUPPOSE IT'LL EVER CATCH ON..."

# DEFUSING A FIZZY BOMB

**Everyone knows what happens when you shake a can of fizzy drink... but now you can do it safely.**

## YOU WILL NEED

Can of fizzy drink
Something to hit it with,
eg ruler

Once you've practised this on your own, you'll be able to do it close up to others and give them a scare.

Shake the can well, then shake it some more for good measure.

Now simply tap it firmly about five times. When you open it, there will be hardly any fizz.

When you shake the drink, bubbles move up to the top of the liquid. Normally , when you open it, the bubbles shoot out of the top, taking the drink with them.

But when you tap the can, all the bubbles burst inside it. So when you open the can, they can't shoot out taking the liquid with them.

Easy!

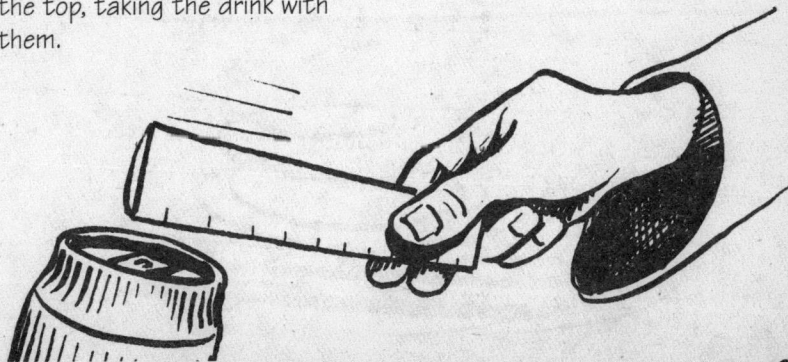

# THE RATTLEBACK

**This is surely one of the greatest mysteries of physics.**

## YOU WILL NEED

300 mm ruler
Plastic teaspoon
Blu-tack

Cut the handle off the spoon, leaving just the bowl.

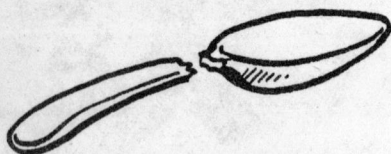

Fill the bowl with Blu-tack – in fact overfill it.

Stick it to the flat side of the ruler.

It must be in the centre, so the ruler balances perfectly, and it must be angled at about 5°–10°. Make sure the rattleback balances level, and none of the corners hits the table.

It is so simple, yet what it does is extraordinary. If you spin it in one direction it will rotate happily until it runs out of energy.

However if you spin it the other way, it will slow down rapidly until it stops, then start spinning in the opposite direction.

Do you know why this happens? If not, you are in good company. Most top scientists are equally puzzled.

# TIPPLE-TOPS

**Another stunningly simple miracle with a stunningly complicated explanation.**

## YOU WILL NEED

Table tennis ball
Water
Paints or felt tip pens

Make a small hole in the ball — just big enough to allow you to pour water in.

Paint the bottom half.

Pour water into the ball, slightly under half-way up.

Place it in the freezer compartment of your fridge.

When the water has frozen solid, take it out again and spin very rapidly like a top, ice-side down.

The top will turn upside down as it spins, until the ice is on top.

Some of the greatest scientists of the century have been puzzled by this seemingly simple problem — why is it easier for the tipple-top to spin with the weight on top?

"IT WORKS!"

23

# BRILLIANT BRIGHT BIG BANG BLOOMERS

These flowers will last for ever.

Paper
Scissors
Green garden stick
Old bowl
Oil paint
Vegetable oil
Sticky tape
Green paper

**1** Cut a strip of paper, about as long as a postcard and half as wide.

**2** Cut strips into it at 1–2cm intervals, 2 cm deep.

**3** Stroke the strips once between your thumb and a hard edge (such as a ruler). This will make them curl like petals.

**4** Attach one end to a green stick, using sticky tape, and wrap the strip around the stick.

**5** Wrap green paper around the base of the flower, so it looks like a real flower stem.

**6** Find an unwanted bowl and half fill it with water.

**7** Mix some oil paint with some oil, and pour onto the water. It will float to the surface.

**8** Swirl the liquid around a little in the bowl then quickly dip the flower into it. It will be coloured with a fine marbled pattern.

Make several flowers. You can mix different colours together to make some truly outrageous blooms.

# COIL MOBILES

These mobiles are very simple to make, and beautiful to watch.

Card
Scissors
Pens, crayons or paints
Thread
Plate

Draw a circle on a piece of thin card by drawing round a dinner plate. Cut out the circle and decorate with swirly patterns.

Cut into the card, going round the edge but a couple of centimetres in. Keep on cutting round, staying always the same distance from the edge, until you are quite close to the centre. Punch a hole in the centre and attach a piece of thread. Hang the mobile over a radiator. and watch it spin magically.

The heat given off by the radiator rises and pushes against the slope on the coiled mobile, pushing it round.

**Warning**: be careful where you hang your mobiles — make sure they can't fall into a fire or heater.

"IT'S MY MOBILE HOME."

# RAINBOW LIGHT SHOW

**Have you ever really *really* seen the amazing colours on a soap bubble? This is how to do it.**

## YOU WILL NEED

Bubble mix (about 2/3 water, 1/3 washing-up liquid, plus a little glycerine if possible)

Black bin liner

Tracing paper, grease-proof paper or kitchen parchment

Straw, to blow bubbles with

Sticky tape

Tape a piece of bin liner (about the size of an A4 sheet of paper) to the table.

Make a cone with the tracing paper and sticky tape. Cut the base so that it is straight. Make sure there's a hole in the top to look through.

Mix up the bubble solution, as above.

Use some to wet the bin liner, so the bubble won't burst.

Use a straw to blow a bubble onto the bin liner.

Cover the bubble carefully with the cone and view through it — you'll get the best results if you have a strong light to the side.

The weird and wonderful rainbow colours are caused by interference between light reflections off the front and the back of the bubble's skin. As the thickness of the skin varies, so the colour changes.

# MAKING PAPER

Here's how to make your own designer paper for notes and cards.

## YOU WILL NEED

Old paper, (eg from news-
papers, magazines, etc)
Dish cloths such as J Cloths
Liquidiser – and a grown-up
Washing-up bowl
Piece of mesh from motor
supply shop (used to patch
car bodies) – about A4 size

**1** Tear up the old newspaper
into stamp-sized pieces; you'll
need about three cupfuls of
these.

**2** Ask a grown-up to help
with the next bit – put about a
handful of paper into a liquidiser,
with twice as much water.
Liquidise for about 30 seconds,
then empty the pulp into the
bowl. Repeat until all the paper
has been pulped.

**3** Prepare a pile of
newspapers with a dish
cloth laid over it.

**4** Slide the mesh into the
pulp, then lift it up, keeping it
level. There should be a thin skin
of pulp all over it.

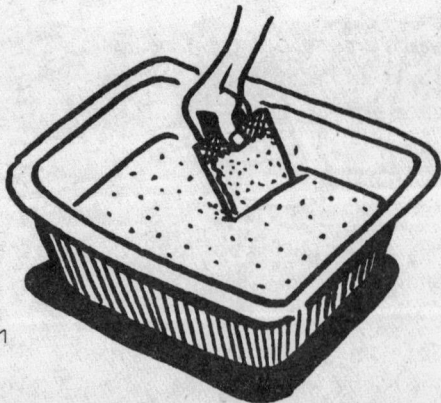

**5** Let it drip over the bowl for a few seconds then transfer it to the pile of newspapers with the dish cloth on top.

**6** Turn the paper out onto the dish cloth, lifting the mesh off carefully so that the sheet of pulp is intact. Lay a dish cloth over it. Repeat until all the pulp is used up, and you have a number of little sheets of wet paper, separated by cloths.

less if it's put in a warm place —then the paper is ready to use.

You can add things to the pulp — pieces of different coloured paper, glitter, pulped grass or leaves — and make really classy personalised paper for letters or cards.

**7** Let the pulp dry. This will take a couple of days — slightly

Dear Gareth
Sorry about the
newspaper

# STRANGE BUT TRUE

## GETTING AHEAD – THE INVENTION OF THE TELEGRAPH

In 1558 an Italian called Porta noticed that if a piece of amber was rubbed with fur, it then deflected a compass needle. He thought about this little thing, then wrote a book in which he said that if this power could be harnessed, people might send messages to each other over long distances. His idea was greeted in the usual way –

YOU'RE NUTS !!

He was actually right, but far, far ahead of his time. Science had a long way to catch up before his dream could come true.

In 1747, a certain Dr Watson tried to pass an electric charge along some wires he ran across Westminster Bridge. He made his servant hold the other ends, to detect the electricity. The experiment was a success!

ANYTHING?

YES!!

So now the static electric charge could be transmitted along wires as far as was needed.

The battery was invented shortly afterwards. It made electricity much more convenient, and saved cats the bother of having amber rubbed on them all the time! In 1839, Charles Wheatstone and William Cooke sent electric current from a battery along wires, and used it to deflect needles pointing to letters of the alphabet a long way away. At last Porta's dream had come true.

Even then, nobody thought this "telegraph" was much use, and only a few were installed along one or two railway lines. But in 1842 John Tawell, a labourer from Slough, boosted the new invention no end, by committing a murder. As the police closed in on him, he hopped on the fast train to London and imagined he was safe. But if Porta had been 300 years ahead of his time, John Tawell was a couple of years behind his. For as the villain sped towards London, the police sent a message ahead of him by telegraph. As Tawell hopped from the train at Paddington Station, he found the boys in blue waiting for him.

Within a few years there were over 16,000 miles of telegraph wire criss-crossing the country. Soon wires were even laid across (under!) the Atlantic Ocean to America.

# GRUB GRABBER

**A great party game – steal your food from the giant Blunderbore's mouth without him noticing.**

## YOU WILL NEED

Box, eg shoe box
Wire
Torch bulb
Bulb holder (from electrical shop)
Battery (suitable power for the bulb)
Tin foil, eg baking foil.
Metal coat hanger
Sandpaper
Sticky tape, scissors, glue, paperclips, card, paints, etc

**1** Cut a hole in the box to form the mouth. Cut a flap in the back of the box, too, so that you can reach into it. Paint a hideous face on the top, around the mouth.

**2** Line the edge of the mouth with a long strip of foil, sticking it in place with glue or double-sided tape.

**3** Attach one end of a piece of wire to the foil with a paper clip. Run the wire down the side of the box inside and tape it. Run the wire out of the box through a hole in the corner and connect the other end to the bulb holder.

**4** Connect another piece of wire to the other terminal on the bulb holder. Connect the other end of the wire to one contact on the battery.

**5** Now, take the coat hanger and cut it down so it's about 30cm long. You'll need to smooth off the cut ends with the sandpaper, and rub off any varnish, too. (You may need grown-up help for this.) Bend the end of the coat-hanger into a hook-shape.

**6** Connect a wire to the other end of the coat-hanger and run that to the remaining contact on the battery.

If the wires are all connected properly, touching the hook to the foil mouth will light the bulb.

**7** You'll need some food to put into the box. Cut card into food shapes, open out some paperclips into loops, and tape the loops to the food. Finish decorating the food and the box,

and you're ready to play! Can you hook the food out of the box without the bulb lighting up?

If you give the different food shapes points, you and your friends can compete for the highest score. Remember, if the bulb lights up, those points don't count!

# DOUBLING UP

## Double double, toil and trouble...
## How many times can you fold a piece of paper?

Take a smallish piece of paper and fold it in half as many times as you can. You won't be able to fold it more than eight times. Now take a really big piece, like a page from a large newspaper, and try again. How many times do you think you can fold it now? Ten? Twenty? Thirty?

You'll find that it is completely impossible to fold the paper more than eight times. And it doesn't matter how big a sheet you use.

Every time you fold the bundle in half you double the thickness, so the thickness increases very rapidly. If you could fold

the paper 14 times it would be over a metre thick. Twenty-three folds and the bundle is nearly a kilometre thick. Thirty folds and it's over 100km thick. Forty-two folds, and it would be wedged between the earth and the moon!

You don't believe it, do you! Well see for yourself. Find a calculator. If we say the thickness of a piece of paper is a tenth of a millimetre, that is 0.0000001 of a kilometre, so punch in 0.0000001. Multiply by 2, then 2 again and again, and do so 42 times. The distance to the moon is about 385,000 km. Are you there yet?

"ONLY 34 FOLDS TO GO!"

34

# SQUIDGY EGGY

Can you remove the shell from an egg without damaging the egg?
Yes, if you have some vinegar.

## YOU WILL NEED

An egg
A jam jar big enough to
    hold it
Vinegar

Put the egg in the jam jar, then
fill up to the brim with vinegar,
and leave for about 4 days.

The acid in the vinegar dissolves
the hard shell, but not the rest
of the egg. Just inside the shell
is a white skin, which holds the
insides of the egg together. The
egg keeps its normal shape, but
it's wibbly-wobbly, and it's very
strange to hold. You can even
see the yolk in the middle.

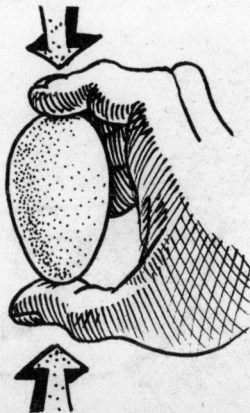

Many animals lay soft eggs; it
must be a lot more comfortable
than laying hard ones. But eggs
with hard shells are safer from
damage.

You can see how strong the shell
of an ordinary egg is if you try
squeezing it end-to-end – it's
very difficult to break the shell.
(Do this over a bowl just in case
you succeed).

Bones are partly made from the
same stuff as egg shells. If you
put a chicken bone in the vinegar,
it will go rubbery after a couple
of days.

# BALANCING BIRD

**This balancing bird seems to defy gravity, hovering over a bottle top.**

## YOU WILL NEED

Paper
Thick card
Scissors
Paints
Two £1 coins
Glue or Blu-tack
Thread

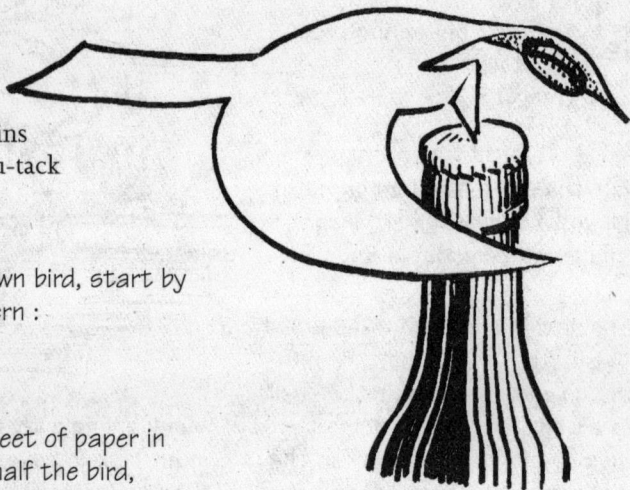

To make your own bird, start by making a pattern :

**1** Fold a sheet of paper in half and draw half the bird, making sure that the wings stretch well in front of the beak. Allow for a long tail.

**2** Cut round the half bird design. When you open the paper out, you'll have both halves of the bird nicely symmetrical.

**3** Place this shape on a piece of fairly thick card (eg from a cereal box), and cut round it.

**4** Fold the beak back and fix it in position by stretching a piece of strong thread from it to the bird's chest.

**5** Now the clever bit. You need to sneak some extra weight in front of the bird's beak to counter-balance the weight of the body behind it. So stick two coins on the underside of the wings, as far forward as you can.

**6** Balance it on the bottle top. You can trim the tail for fine adjustments.

## YOU COULD BALANCE TOO – IF YOU DID THIS

# DEFY GRAVITY!

**Make a ball roll uphill.**

## YOU WILL NEED

Shoe box
Match box
Card
Coat hanger
Scissors
Glue
Table tennis ball

**1** Stick the matchbox onto the end of the shoe box (as shown).

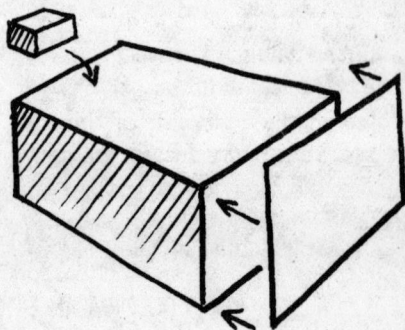

**2** Glue a piece of cardboard at the other end. The top of this should about 1cm higher than the matchbox and level.

**3** Cut down the coat hangers (ask a grown-up to help with this). You want the straight bits, with one end bent down about 1cm. Insert these ends into the matchbox about 1cm apart. The other ends should now rest on the card, and they should be sloping upward.

**4** A small card tab at the end of the rails will stop the ball from wandering off.

**5** Place the table tennis ball on the tracks, resting against the tab.

**6** Now when you slide the tracks apart the ball rolls towards you, apparently defying gravity.

If you look carefully from the side, you can see that the ball is actually rolling downhill, as it sinks between the rails.

If you are clever you can get the ball to roll quite a long way before it drops. Cut a line of holes under the rails and have a competition to see who can roll the ball farthest.

# GRILLER THRILLER

**Inside every grill pan there's a mighty church bell
struggling to get out.**

## YOU WILL NEED

Grill shelf, spoon or wire
  coat-hanger
String

Hang the grill shelf on a length
of string, wrap the string around
your fingers, stick your fingers in
your ears, lean forward so that
the grill swings freely. Now let it
knock gently against a piece of
furniture. It looks daft, but it
sounds amazing! You hear a bell
chiming.

You can get the same sounds
from a spoon, a wire coat-
hanger, almost anything
made of metal.

When you listen to
those metal things
normally, the sound,
which comes at
you through
the air, is a
shapeless
clunk. That clunk
is a mix of high
"chings" and low
"bongs".

When you listen to this hodge-
podge of noise through the
string/finger arrangement, the
soft materials (the string, the
flesh of your fingers) absorb the
high "chings" but transmit the
low "bongs", so all you hear is
the deep bell-like sounds.

This explains why your voice never
sounds right on a tape
recording. Normally you hear your
own voice partly through the
bone of your skull. The tape
recorder only hears it through
the air.

# SNAPPY BIG BANG BANGER

**A shockingly simple shocker.**

## YOU WILL NEED

2 expired credit cards or
  phone cards
Sturdy elastic band, the
  length of a credit card
  or shorter

**1** Check that the card
really is finished with —
you could be in BIG trouble
if you get this wrong.

**2** Cut two notches on
one long side of each card.

**3** Loop the elastic band
over the cards as shown.

**4** Fold the cards back like
closing a book. The elastic bands
should run across the cards
outside — if you're doing it right
it should be quite hard to pull
against the elastic bands.

**5** When you want to make the
bang, just throw the banger in
the air. The elastic will do the
rest. The stronger the elastic,
the bigger the bang.

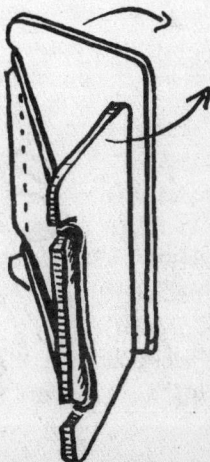

# PIG SONGS

**This musical instrument sounds every bit as melodious as a pig.**

## YOU WILL NEED

Cardboard tube, the bigger
  the better
Balloon, preferably pink
Straw, preferably pink
Strong thread or garden wire
Pink card, paints, scissors,
  glue

**1** Cut the mouth-piece
off the balloon.

**2** Fix the end of the straw
in to the middle of the balloon by
putting a blob of glue on the tip,
pulling the balloon over it, tying
very firmly with the thread or
twisting with the garden wire,
then turning the balloon the
other way up.

**3** Stretch the balloon
to fit over the end of the tube.

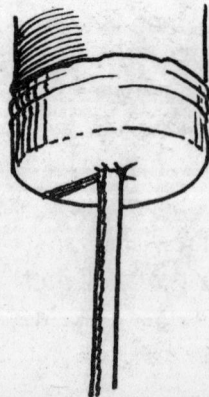

Play by licking fingers and
stroking the straw until piggy
oinks.

To make the pig's body, cut out three pieces of pink card, big enough to wrap around the tube.

Glue one right around the tube. Fix the second so that the middle is glued to the pig's back, but the ends can hang down and be cut to form the legs.

Work out how long you want the head to be, and cut that length from the third piece of card.

Fold into a cone, as shown. Glue together and fold ears down.

Cut a slit at either side and slide onto the body.

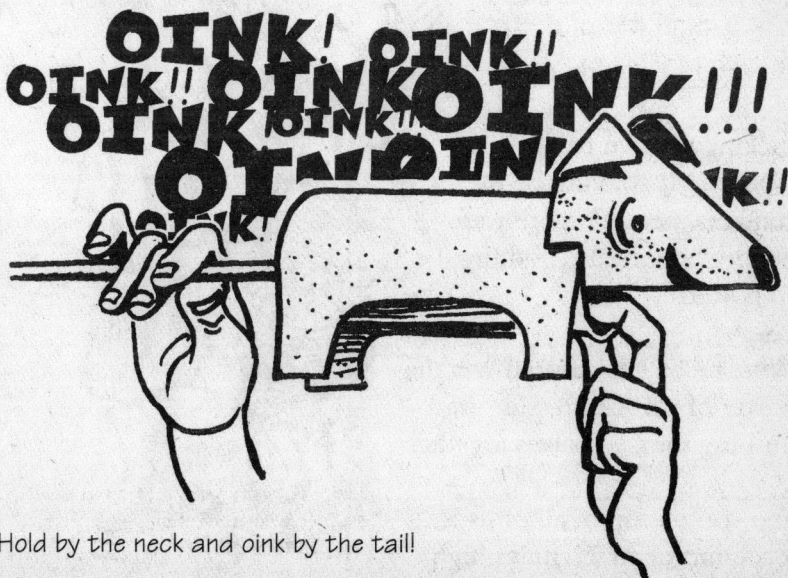

OINK! OINK!!
OINK!! OINK OINK!!!
OINK OINK OINK
OINK OINK!!

Hold by the neck and oink by the tail!

# STRANGE BUT TRUE

## YOU MUST BE COMPLETELY MAGDEBURG!

Otto von Guericke is famous because he spent his life thinking about nothing.

The problem with nothing, is that it isn't easy to find. Nearly everything is full of something. 300 years ago most people thought that the air around us was made of nothing. (It was only later they started to discover that air was actually jam-packed full of oxygen, nitrogen, carbon dioxide, carbon monoxide, sulphur dioxide... you name it.) But air can't be nothing – you only have nothing when you've taken the air away.

In 1654, Von Guericke decided to find out what it's like to have a bowl of nothing.. He built two bronze half-spheres, fixed a valve to one of them, placed them loosely together, then rigged up an air pump and pumped away until everything inside was removed – all the oxygen, nitrogen, everything. He now had a sphere full of nothing at all... and he couldn't get the thing open. What was sticking the two half-spheres together? It couldn't be the contents, because there were none – how could 'nothing' be so powerful?

"BRILLIANT! HOW DID YOU DO IT?"

"IT WAS NOTHING!"

What he had discovered was the power of air. Air pressure was pushing the two halves together.

You see, on top of all of us is a column of air 22 miles high, stretching to the edge of space, and though air is not heavy in small amounts, 22 miles of it adds up to a fair weight – how much, Von Guericke was about to find out.

His attempts to get the half-spheres apart became increasingly desperate. In the end it took two teams of eight horses to separate them.

"ANY LUCK YOUR END?"

"NEIGH!"

The "Magdeburg Sphere" became so famous that even the Emperor travelled to Magdeburg... to see absolutely nothing!

"WHATEVER'S IN THERE, I WANT SOME NEW CLOTHES MADE FROM IT"

EMPEROR

# MAGDEBURG SPHERETTES

**You can do Otto von Guericke's experiment... without the horses!**

## YOU WILL NEED

Two identical glasses – the bigger the better
Newspaper
Hot water – the hotter the better, but not too hot for your fingers!
Cold water – the colder the better

Put three pieces of paper together and cut or tear to be slightly wider than the tops of the glasses. This will be the seal between the glasses. Tear a hole in the middle and soak the paper in water for a minute or so.

Pour very hot water into the two glasses. Leave it there for about half a minute so the glass gets nice and hot.

Pour the water out, then place the two glasses in the sink, mouth to mouth, with the seal between them, as in the picture. Just before you finally position them, hold them a little apart. The hot glasses will warm up the air inside, some of which will be forced out as it expands.

When you finally place the glasses together, make sure their mouths are perfectly in line all round. Press gently together.

Pour the cold water over the whole thing. The air inside will cool, contract slightly, and the two glasses will be sucked together.

It's only a shadow of the suction that Otto von Guericke managed, but you just try getting those glasses apart!

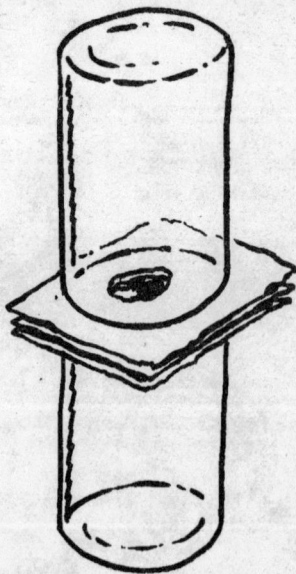

# INSTANT UGLY MUGS

Turn beautiful people, like Gareth, into really horrifying people, like.... well, like Gareth.

## YOU WILL NEED

A picture of your victim's face
A pair of scissors

Cut out the eyes and mouth, and simply put them back upside down. The picture will look very spooky.

Strangely, if you turn the whole thing on its head it won't look spooky any more. When we look at a face we pay particular attention to the eyes and mouth. So long as those look OK, the rest doesn't bother us so much, even when it's all topsy turvy!

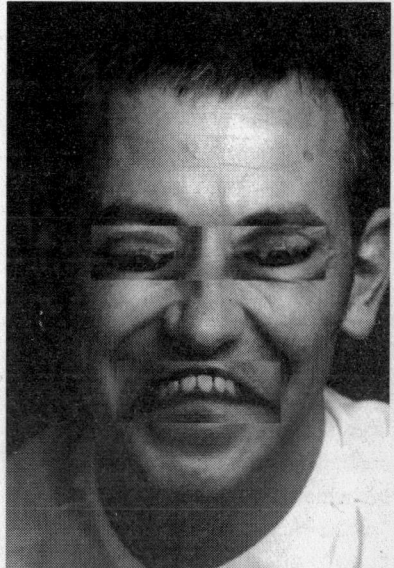

47

# MEGA COLOUR CHANGE

**This is a stunning optical illusion.**

## YOU WILL NEED

A thick marker pen,
   preferably one that does
   lines about 5mm thick
A ruler
Card or paper
Fine scissors OR
Sharp knife, chopping board
   and grown-up

**1** Use the marker pen and
ruler to draw straight lines
across the sheet of card or
paper. The gap between the lines
should be the same thickness as
the lines themselves.

(If you have a computer and
printer in the house, a grown-up
may be able to find a way to do
the grid automaticallyfor you).

**2** Draw two squares at
either side of the grid. Cut out
the black stripes from one
square and the white stripes
from the other. The best way to
do this is to get a grown up to
slice them out using a very
sharp knife, ruler and cutting
board, but small scissors can do
as well.

**3** Now put the paper on a
sheet of coloured paper, or anything that's coloured. One of the
squares will look darker than the
other. Turn the grid around and
the effect is reversed.

The human eye isn't able to work
out that the colour is different
from the stripe; it "adds" the
colour to the white to "see" light
colour, and adds the colour to
the black to see dark colour. In
the same way you "see" a grey
background in the illustration
opposite, even though it's actually black dots on white paper.

Incidentally, both those greys
opposite are the same!

# FOTO FLICK BOOK

**You've probably come across the usual flick book;
here is an interesting variation.**

Camera
Roll of film, preferably 36
   frames

Be brave! Be reckless! You are about to use up a whole roll of film in one go.

Choose an interesting scene to "film". Fix the camera to point at the same place, then take snap after snap, at regular intervals, until the film is finished.

When the film is developed, arrange them in a stack. When you flick through them you'll see a moving picture, just like a film.

Remember that because of the way the pictures are held, the left side of the pictures will be largely lost — make sure the most interesting bit is on the right side.

*Suggestions for scenes to film:*

A train coming into a station. Take one picture every second, starting when the train is almost in. Point along the platform. (This is the scene shown in one of the very first films, almost exactly 100 years ago.)

Sunset, especially sunset at the seaside. Start filming just before the sun touches the horizon and take a picture every minute. Reverse the order of the pictures and you have sunrise.

The busy beach One shot every second.

Set up your own scene with friends moving from one position to another.

# 3-D PICTURES

**Make your own stereoscopic snaps.**

To make a 3-D picture, you need to photograph a view as each eye sees it. So take a picture, then move the camera about 8cm to the right and snap exactly the same view again.

When the pictures are developed, pick the most interesting part of the view (with the most depth to the shot), and cut identical 4cm wide strips from each picture.

Set up for viewing as below, sticking the left hand picture to left and the right hand shot to right.

Hold the second piece of card (about A4 sized), as above, down the centre between the two pictures and between your two eyes. Make sure it casts no shadows. Each eye can see only one picture.

Let your eyes de-focus - stare into the distance - and the two pictures will seem to move together, overlapping and finally blending into one stereoscopic picture of your view.

Although the two pictures appear the same, your mind will spot tiny differences which your eyes cannot!

# RICE LEVITATION

**You've never seen levitating rice before? Well, have a stab at this!**

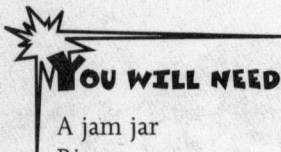

## YOU WILL NEED

A jam jar
Rice
A pen or pencil

Fill a jam jar with rice. Push a pencil into it. When you lift the pencil, does the rice rise with it? Not yet; but it will soon!

First shake the jar gently for half a minute. The rice will settle in the jar, and you can pour some more in. Now push the pencil in again.

And again, and again.

And again and again and again, and keep doing that until suddenly, when you lift the pencil, the jar comes up with it.

Amazing!

Every time you push the pencil in, the rice grains are packed a little tighter together. Eventually they are so tight-packed that one last push of the pencil squeezes them all against the side of the jar and the pencil is gripped.

# TAME TWISTER

**Make a tornado in a bottle**

Water
Drop of washing-up liquid
Large jar, eg coffee jar, or
  round storage jar. It must
  have clear sides.

Simply three-quarters fill the jar with water, add the drop of washing up liquid and close the lid.

When you swirl the bottle round, the tornado is formed in the middle.

The shape is very similar to the real tornados that sweep across the southern states of the USA every year.

"DON'T SHAKE IT QUITE
SO HARD NEXT TIME"

# GOOD DOG

**Good Dog sits up and begs all by himself.**

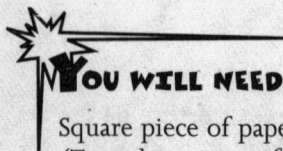

Square piece of paper.
(To make a square from a
piece of paper, see page
95.)

**1** Fold the square across
from corner to corner to give you
the diagonal centre line. Unfold.

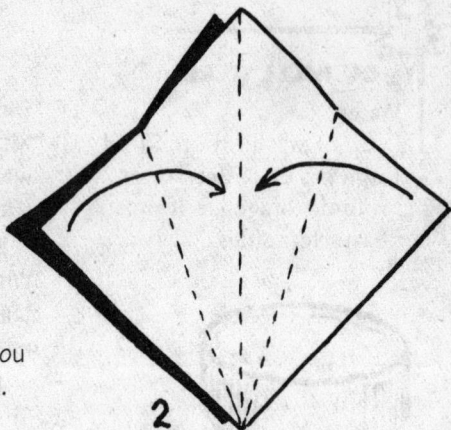

**2** Fold left and right sides
into the centre line, to give a kite
shape.

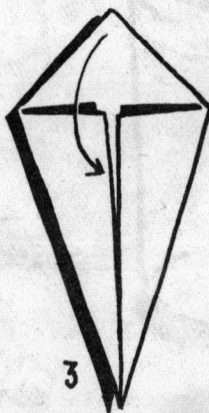

**3** Fold the top corner down,
to give a triangle.

**4** Fold the two top corners
down to touch the centre line,
giving you a kite shape again.

54

**5** Fold the top of the kite down, to give a triangle again.

**6** Fold the outside corners in again, to give another kite shape.

**7** Fold the whole thing across the middle.

**8** Draw the dog on each side.

**9** To make your dog perform, fold it tightly and place nose down on the table. As the shape opens out, it will suddenly jump up and beg.

If it begs too soon, press the crease more firmly. If it's too slow, check that the flaps on the inside are pushing against each other.

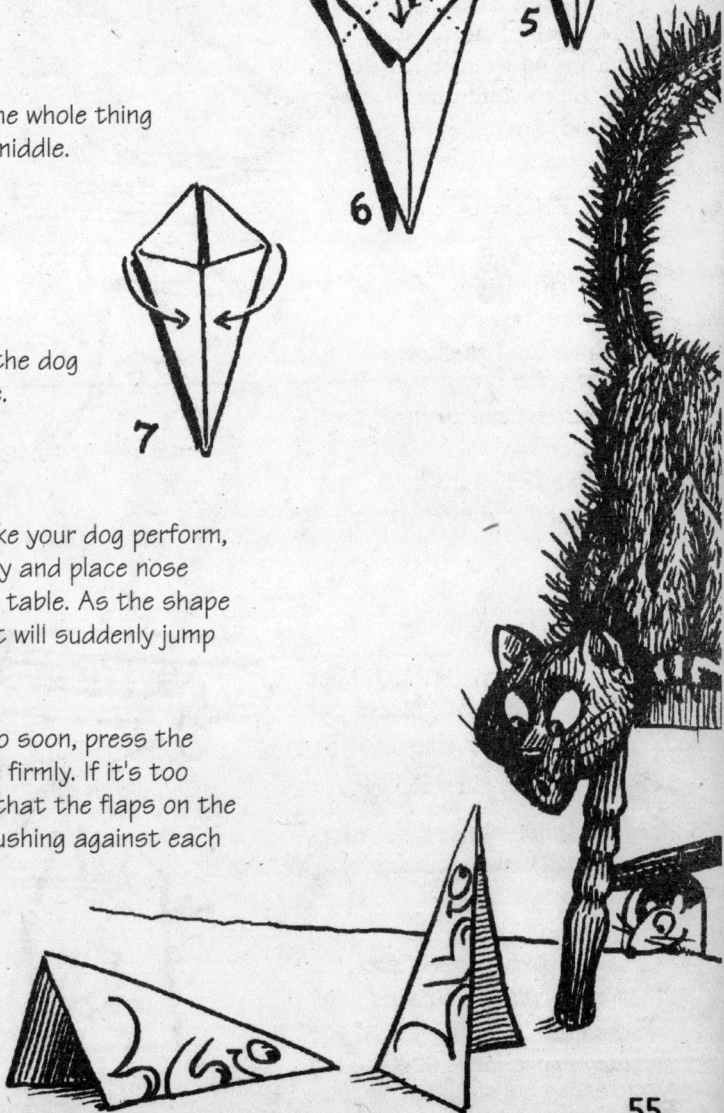

# LAND YACHT

**So light, it races away in the slightest breeze.**

## YOU WILL NEED

Two 30cm rulers
3 small plant pot trays
Knitting needle
3 plastic building bricks or
  lolly sticks
3 cocktail sticks
Plastic bag
Drink straw
2 paper clips
2 elastic bands
Strong thread
Tape, Cool-melt glue,
  card
Grown-up with drill

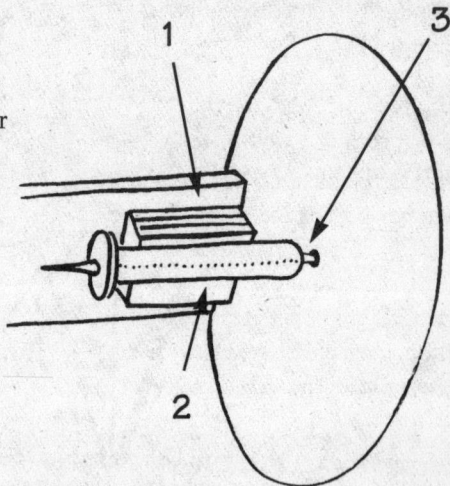

Assemble the yacht by attaching the rulers with elastic bands.

TO BUILD THE WHEELS:

Find three plastic bricks, about 3 x 2 x 1 cm or make blocks by glueing the lolly sticks together, then cutting the block into three.

Stick one block in position on the ruler (1).

Cut a straw to extend about 1/2cm beyond the outside edge of the block, and flush with the inside edge. Glue it in place (2).

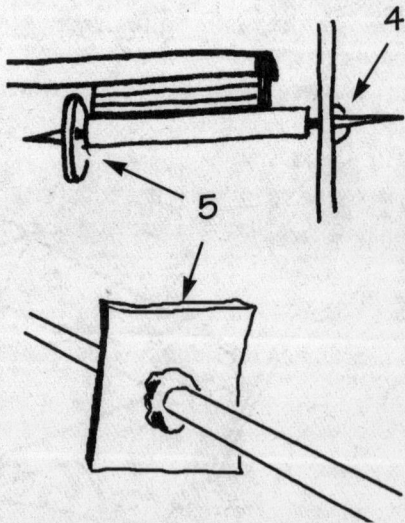

Drill a small hole in the centre of the "wheel" (plant pot tray) (3).

Insert the cocktail stick and glue on the outside (ie bowl side)(4).

Insert the stick into the straw. Cut a small piece of plastic or card to act as a washer on the inner end(5). Glue if necessary.

Repeat this operation for each wheel, in the positions shown below.

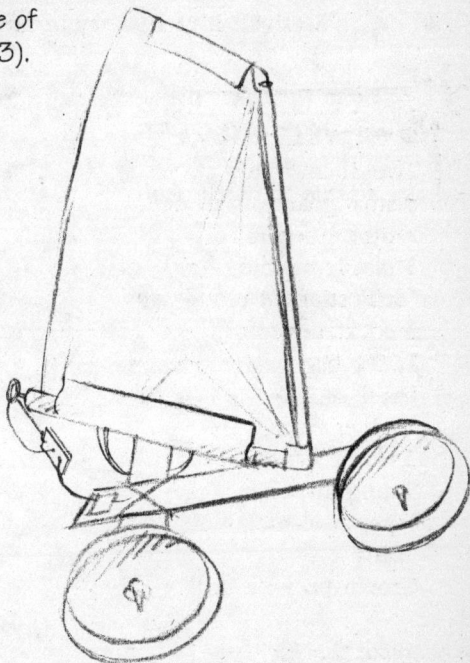

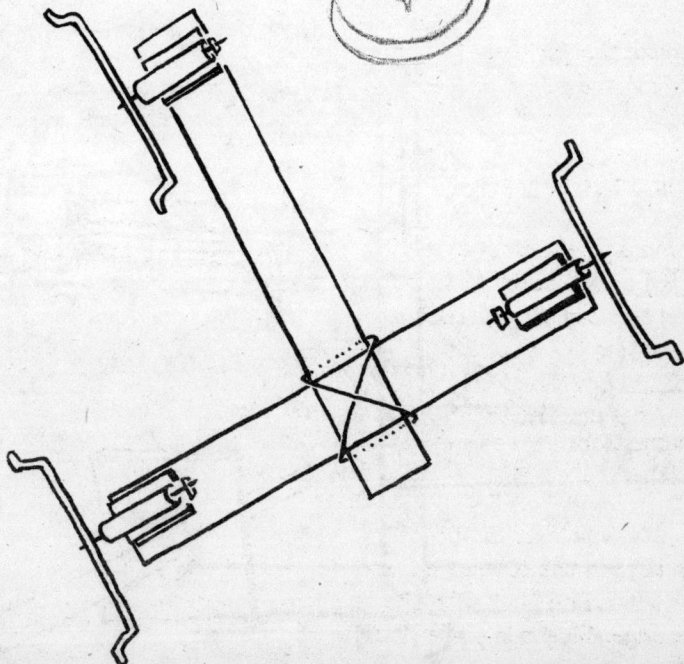

## SAIL

Drill a hole in the ruler with one wheel attached – about 10cm from the wheel end – for the knitting needle to fit through. Glue it in position.

Open out a paperclip and tape one end to the top of the knitting needle, bending the rest down to form the top arm of the sail.

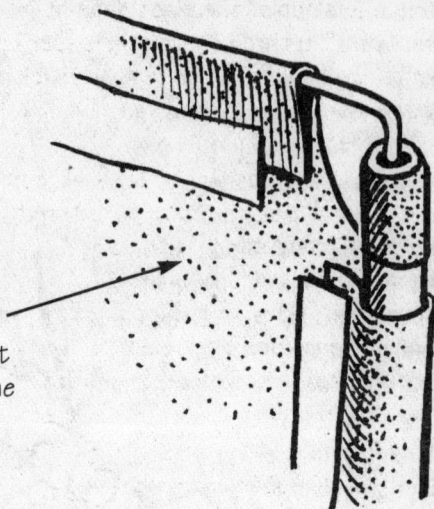

Open out a paper clip into a loop, and stick it to one end of the pencil. Tape the other end of the pencil to the bottom of the mast.

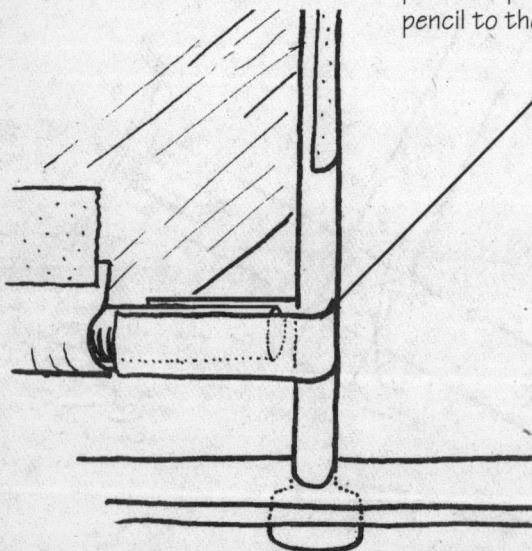

Cut a sail out of the plastic, to fit into the gap between the three spars (the paper clip, the knitting needle and the pencil). Stick into place with tape.

To adjust the position of the sail, cut out a small piece of card, poke three holes in it and string a thread from the back of the yacht through it, through the loop on the pencil and back, as shown. You can change the length of the thread – and the position of the sail – by moving the card along the thread.

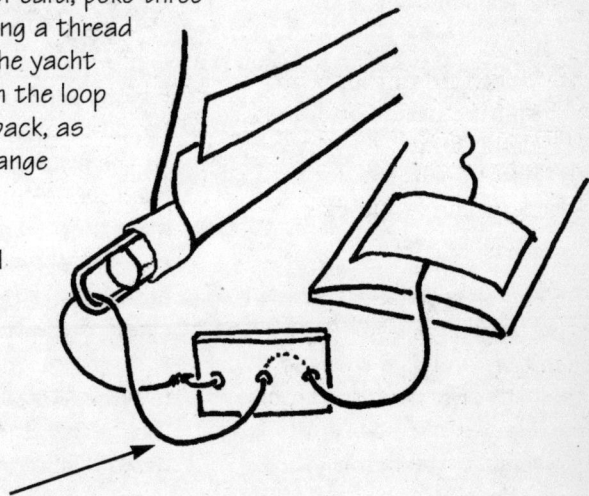

# HARMONOGRAPH

**Draw stunning patterns with this device.**

2 chairs and 2 brooms
String
Seed tray
Book
Thick card or thin board
Knitting needle or dowel
Elastic band
Felt-tip pen
Plasticene or Blu-tack
Kebab skewer

The set-up is as shown. Sling equal lengths of string under the seed tray and glue them to it. Hang the tray from the broom handles. Put the book in the tray to weight it; the heavier the book, the longer the tray will swing.

Stick a piece of thick flat card over the top. The drawing paper is attached to that.

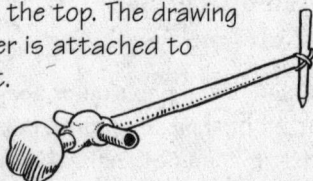

For the pen arm, use elastic bands to attach a felt-tip pen to the front end of a knitting needle. Use cool-melt glue to stick a straw across the other end. The skewer runs through the straw and is fixed to a support close to the tray, eg. books, so the pen presses lightly on the middle of the card, but can ride up or down. The plasticene acts as a counterweight.

When the tray is swung, the pen draws beautiful patterns.

# STRANGE BUT TRUE

## DYEING TO FIND OUT

Brightening up your clothes with a little colour isn't new. Almost as soon as our ancestors started weaving cloth, eight thousand years ago, people began putting colour in their clothes – by accident.

"UG!" *

It wasn't long before people started staining their clothes on purpose. The most popular way was by boiling their stone-age T-shirts up with the woad plant, a common weed related to the nettle. This made a nice bright blue colour.

*TRANSLATED – "HOW DO YOU EXPECT ME TO GET THESE GRASS STAINS OUT?"

Those who wanted to be different, and who had lots of money, went for a more exotic dye, made from the extremely rare and expensive purpura shellfish. The colour was called purple, and for thousands of years purple was the colour that meant "I AM VERY RICH!". It is still known as the colour of emperors.

"EITHER STOP MY PURPLE FROM RUNNING OR INVENT THE UMBRELLA"

But there was no point getting your kit done out in pricy purple if all the colour rinsed out the first time you washed it.

This has always been a problem. Even nowadays we haven't completely solved it: how many times has the washing come out grey – or worse, pink or green – because someone's shirt "ran" in the wash? But it used to be much more of a problem, until some ancient Romans made the most unlikely discovery.

Science often advances by lucky accidents. This was one of the luckiest. A group of dyers found that their colours stayed fixed if they soaked their garments in a mixture of shale (a type of rock), seaweed and urine (pee).

How on earth did they find this out? Maybe the dyeing pit was made of shale, and perhaps the sea washed in and left some seaweed and possibly one of the workers was so desperate to go to the toilet, he had a pee in the pit... We will never know, we can only guess. But whoever spotted it, and worked out how to do it again and again, we owe them a big thank–you.

"BACK TO WORK!"

"HANG ON; I'M JUST CHANGING THE COURSE OF HISTORY."

Urine was an important part of the dye-fixing business until very recently. In fact the people in the houses around the dye works were paid for their pee, which was collected in buckets every morning.

Nowadays we use Alum, which does the same thing.

For two thousand years woad and its blue colour was by far the easiest and cheapest way to dye cloth – that's why army and navy uniforms were nearly always blue. Huge factories sprang up, dedicated to using that one colour.

In the 1950s new chemicals made a variety of new colours cheaply available. The "psychedelic" designs of the 60s had little use for blue, so a lot of blue-dye workers lost their jobs. No doubt this left them feeling blue.

They were rescued by the development of their new secret weapon – blue jeans! Nowadays, thanks to jeans, blue dye is as much in demand as ever it was.

And the future may belong to woad. For an environmentally friendly blue ink is being developed for laser printers – from the plant that set us all on the right woad in the first place!

# HELLO GOOD DYE

**Dye your own clothes.**

White T-shirt (or another
  item of white clothing)
Alum (available from
  chemists)
Two large bowls
Hot water
Sieve
Vegetables of your choice:
yellow onion skins
  for yellow
red onion skins for
  brown/green
red cabbage for
  purple/blue
beetroot for red

The alum acts as a fixer. This
means it "sticks" the dye to the
fabric. Without the fixer the
colour would run out the first
time you washed your T-shirt.

Dissolve a tablespoon of alum in
a large bowl of hot water and
soak the T-shirt in it for an hour.
Allow the shirt to dry.

To make the dye, chop up the vegetable of your choice into small pieces and soak in hot water for 15 minutes. Pour the mixture into another bowl through the sieve to get rid of the bits. You have made your dye.

Soak the T-shirt in it for 15 minutes, then allow to dry.

PRIDE

TIE-DYED PRIDE

You can make "tie-dye" patterns by wrapping the cloth round a coin and tying an elastic band round it (do that several times for a repeated pattern), before you put the cloth into the dye.

Wear your newly dyed T-Shirt with pride.

# WIRE FLYER

**Odin, king of the Norse gods, had a flyingboat –
here's how to make one.**

## YOU WILL NEED

Drinking straw
Kebab skewer or plant stick
Fishing line
Card
Plasticene
Cool-melt glue
Scissors

Cut the
ship's body
and sail out of
the card. The body
could be 15cm long, and
the sail about 15 x 10 cm.

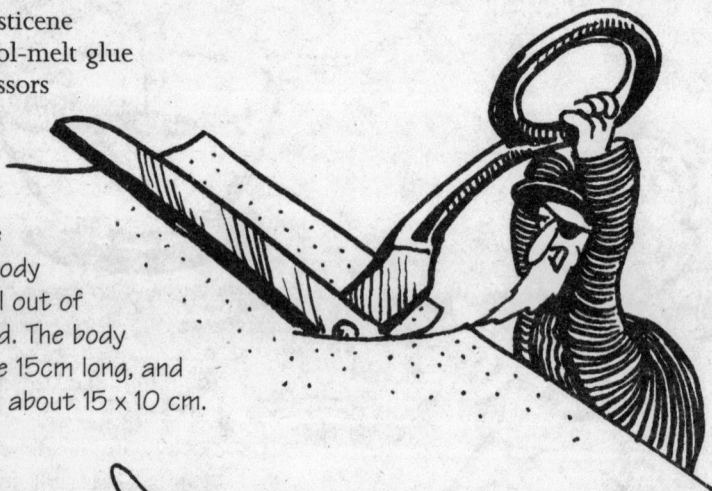

Paint them with stripes,
shields, etc.

Use the cool-melt glue to stick the straw along the back of the boat.

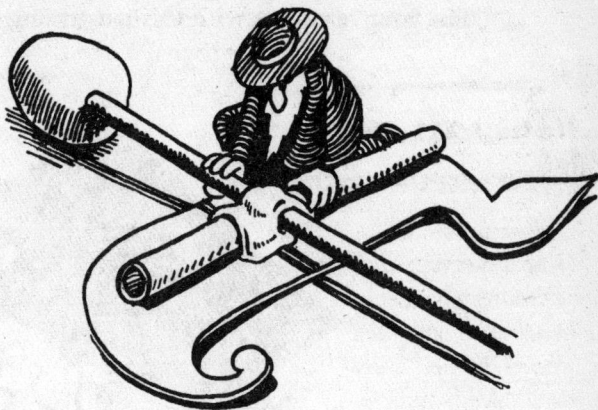

Now glue the kebab skewer across that - use plenty of glue to bulk it out. Use the top part as a mast for the sail. Put plasticene on the bottom as a counterweight, to keep the boat upright.

Thread the fishing line through the straw, then fix tightly across your room or garden.

Blow on the sail to make Odin's boat fly.

# TOO SLOW!

Test your reactions with this frustrating game.

**YOU WILL NEED**

A five pound note

Borrow a five pound note from a grown-up; tell them it's only for a second. Immediately offer to give it back — they just have to catch it!

Hold it just above their open fingers, and tell them to grab it as soon as you let go.

They won't be able to! The fiver will drop through their hand before their fingers have started moving.

68

This shows how slow human reactions are. When you drop the note, their eyes spot your hand opening and send a message to the brain, which sends another message down the arm to the hand, which snaps shut. But it takes so long for all that to happen that the note is already well on its way to the floor.

To make the grown-up feel better about how slow they are, swap around. Your reactions are just as slow as theirs.

Motorists have to keep a safe distance from the car in front to allow for this half second reaction time if the car in front brakes suddenly.

"THIS TIME I'LL CATCH IT...
THIS TIME..."

# THE BIG PUFF

Take all the huffing and puffing out of candle blowing
with this handy scientific gadget.

## YOU WILL NEED

A cardboard tube, like the
  ones some crisps come in
A burst balloon
An elastic band

**1** Cut the bottom off the
tube.

**2** Stretch the balloon over
the end, holding it in place with
the elastic band.

**3** Cut a hole slap bang in the
centre of the plastic lid, about
1cm across and nice and round.

**4** Put the lid on the tube.

**5** Point it at a candle. Tap the balloon, and a powerful puff of air will shoot out of the front and blow the candle out.

Usually when you blow, the wind comes out of your mouth in all directions and fades away pretty fast. The hole in the tube holds the power of the puff together in a spinning ring of air.

You can see this action if you insert an incense stick in the hole for a few seconds, enough to fill the tube with smoke. When you tap the balloon the smoke is puffed out in a spinning hoop – smoke rings!

See from how far you can blow the candle out.

Oh, by the way, Happy birthday!

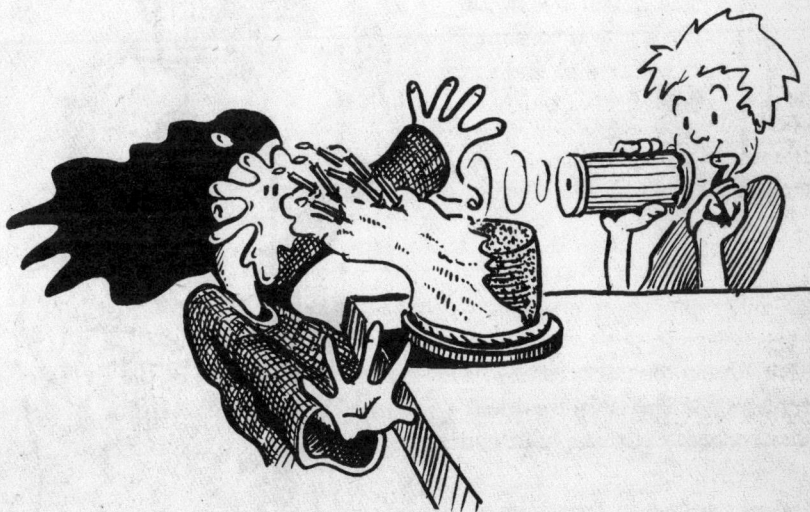

# CARTESIAN DIVER

**This diver will obey your every command.**

3cm length of straw
Plastic drink bottle (1 litre),
   filled with water
Blu-tack

As you squeeze the bottle, everything in it gets squashed, including the air in the straw. Because it is squashed into a smaller space, the air bubble is smaller, and the buoyancy is reduced, so the diver dives.

Bung up the top end of the straw with a little Blu-tack. Wrap a dollop of Blu-tack round the bottom end. You must adjust this weight by lowering the straw into a basin of water and adding or subtracting Blu-tack until the straw floats upright just below the surface.

When you've got the weight roughly right, transfer your straw diver to the bottle filled with water. You will probably have to readjust the weight – the diver should float slowly upwards.

Screw the top on firmly. When you squeeze the bottle, the diver will sink to the bottom. Releasing the bottle brings him up again.

Squeeze and release as you give him orders. He will obey you!

72

# STRANGE BUT TRUE
## THE MAN WHO KEPT BOUNCING BACK –
## CHARLES GOODYEAR.

Here's a man with one mega-obsession.

Charles Goodyear was an American, born in 1800. He was poor, but he was determined to make himself rich by solving the age-old problem of perishing rubber.

Rubber had been bouncing around for thousands of years; in South America the Aztecs had found out how to make rubber balls, boots and bottles before the rest of the world had even found out how to get to South America.

"HMM; SOMEONE NEEDS TO INVENT A BETTER SIZE."

When the rest of the world was introduced to rubber, they really took to it – it was light, bendy, waterproof, cheap, easy to mould into interesting shapes. Joseph Priestley (the father of fizzy drinks) discovered it was even good at rubbing out pencil marks – that's how it got the name "rubber".

EUROPE'S FIRST CONTACT WITH SOUTH AMERICA

"CAN WE HAVE OUR BALL BACK PLEASE?"

But rubber had a big problem – it didn't last. In cold weather it went too hard, in hot weather it went too soft, and quite soon it "perished" – became sticky and dropped apart.

If only, thought Goodyear, if only a magic ingredient could be added that kept it just right. This dream obsessed him. As he experimented with various mixtures he became poorer and poorer, knowing that when he got it right he would be very rich.

**SPLOT!**

"NOT MUCH USE FOR BASKET BALL THEN."

He had no education and almost no equipment. He was often thrown into prison for debt and everybody laughed at him, but still he bounced back.

"YOUR CHEQUE BOUNCED!"

"DON'T TROUBLE ME NOW..."

He tried adding sulphur to the mix, and got close to solving the problem, but then he accidentally dropped the finished piece of rubber on the fire. When he rescued it he noticed something – between the burnt bit and the untouched bit there was a tiny layer of rubber that was exactly right. So that was the answer – add sulphur and heat it.

"THERE, RUBBER WHEELS ON YOUR CART. HOW DOES IT LOOK?"

"IT LOOKS TYRED."

Thanks to his persistence and acute observation, Charles Goodyear had invented "metallic gum elastic". (He later called it "vulcanised rubber" after the Roman God of fire, Vulcan.)

Nowadays vulcanised rubber is used in everything from car tyres to cricket bats.

But did Goodyear get rich? No, all those people who had laughed at him before suddenly wanted to steal his invention for themselves, and he spent the next twenty years trying to fight them off before he died, still poor, still in debt, in 1860.

# UNBURSTABLE BALLOONS

**When you stick a needle into a balloon it bursts...
but not if you know this trick.**

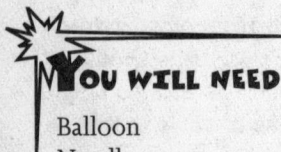

Balloons burst because the rubber is tightly stretched — the smallest hole causes it to rip catastrophically.

Stick a small piece of sticky tape to the balloon and it won't tear there.

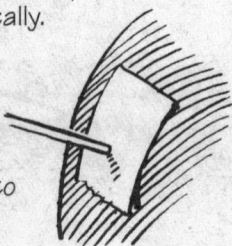

You can stick the needle through the sticky tape patch.

But remember, the most important part of this trick is the wind-up. Nobody likes the sound of balloons bursting. Make them suffer before you perform your miracle.

# BUBBLE PING PONG

**The slowest game of table tennis in the world.**

Balloon
Bubble-blowing liquid

This may be better with two of you; one blows a soap bubble, while the other rubs a balloon briskly on their pullover.

Bring the balloon close to the bubble and it will be strangely attracted to it. With a bit of practice you'll be able to drag the bubble around. With lots of practice you'll be able to play a snail's game of table tennis.

The key to this magic is the electrons which buzz around all the molecules in the universe. By rubbing the balloon you scrape some of its electrons off, and the balloon is attracted to any source of electrons it can find. In fact the balloon is attracting everything in the room ever so slightly, but only the soap bubble is light enough to actually move towards it.

77

# TORTURING SOAP BUBBLES

In case you thought soap bubbles had to be round,
here's a way to force them into some more twisted shapes.

## YOU WILL NEED

Garden wire or
    pipe-cleaners
Washing-up liquid
Bowl
Water
Glycerine (from a
    chemist – not
    essential)

**1** Make some wire frames
from garden wire or pipe-clean-
ers. The easiest shapes are a
cube and a triangular pyramid.
The sides should be about 5-7cm
long.

**2** Now make a bubble mix
with water and washing-up liquid.
(Adding a little glycerine makes
the bubbles last longer.) You will
need enough to cover the frames.

**3** Now you're ready to torture those bubbles! Dunk the frames in the bubble mix and look at the weird and wonderful curves that appear.

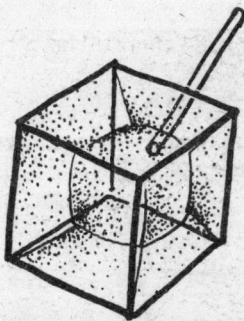

**4** Dip the straw and use it to blow extra bubbles inside the frames. You may even be able to blow a beautifully curved cube within the cube frame. Good luck!

# CAROUSEL

**A merry-go-round that really goes round.**

1 big and 1 small yoghurt pot
Two 20cm foil dishes
2 kebab skewers or garden
  sticks
Cocktail sticks (at least 10)
Elastic band
Glue – cool-melt and PVA
Stiff card, scissors, paints

TO MAKE THE TOP PART:

Cut a 17cm circle out of the card. Make a cut from edge to centre, overlap and glue to form a cone. Stick this to the top dish.

Make 1cm holes in the middle of the foil dishes and the small yoghurt pot. Use cool-melt glue to stick the two dishes to either end of the pot.

Carefully insert eight cocktail sticks evenly around the outside, gluing to top and bottom foil dish.

Cut out eight horses and glue them to the cocktail sticks.

Paint and decorate the carousel. Make it look nice and bright.

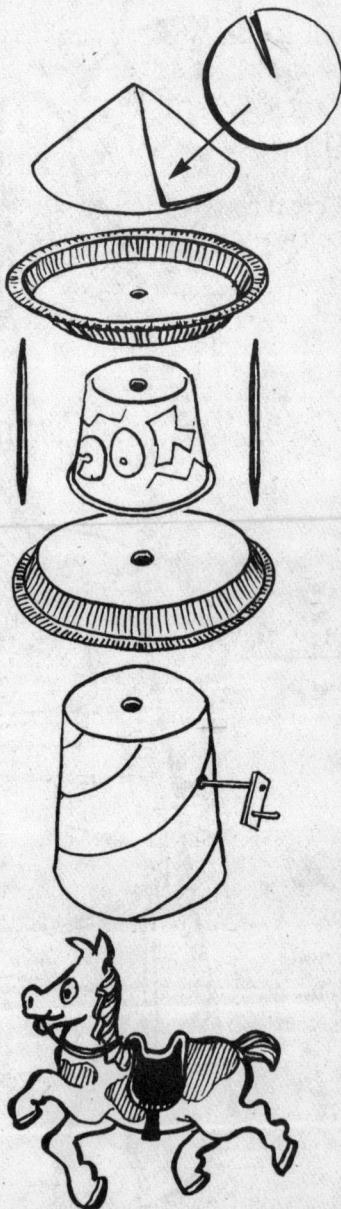

## TO MAKE THE ENGINE:

Cut a rotor wheel (1) out of stiff card. Make it a little smaller than the base of the big yoghurt pot.

Bore a hole through it big enough to take the skewer or stick.

Cut a small (2cm) drive wheel out of stiff card (2). Bore a hole through the middle big enough to take a skewer.

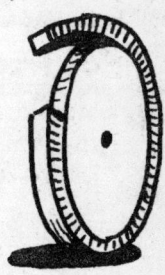

Glue part of an elastic band around the rim.

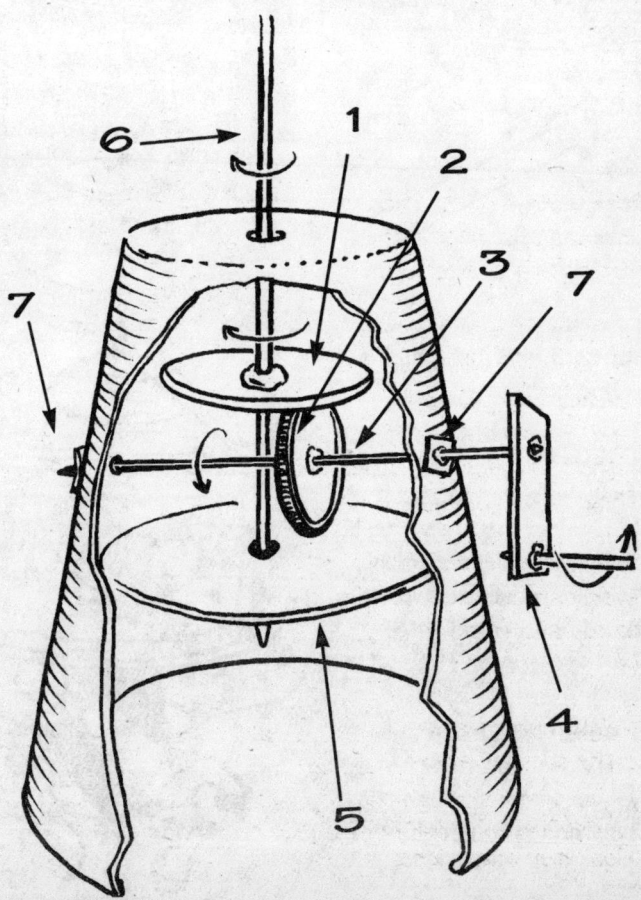

Insert a length of skewer (3) right through the big yoghurt pot from side to side, about 4cm from the base. As it passes through, skewer the drive wheel onto it. Don't glue yet.

Make simple washers out of card and position on the skewer on the outsides of the pot (7). Don't glue yet.

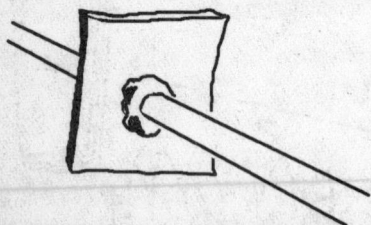

Make a crank as shown (4), with a piece of card and a piece of skewer. Glue firmly.

Prepare the lower guide plate for gluing firmly into the pot as shown (5), below the drive wheel. Bore a hole in the centre of this, and in the centre of the top of the yoghurt pot, only slightly wider than the skewer.

For final assembly, insert the skewer (6) down through the top of the yoghurt pot, through the rotor wheel and through the

guide plate. The other end goes up through the carousel and sits in the point of the roof.

Line up the rotor wheel and drive wheel. Then glue these wheels into place on the skewers, and then the washers in place on the outside of the pot.

Stick the guide plate into place, resting on the inside of the pot, so it stops the skewer (6) from wobbling around. The rotor wheel presses down on the drive wheel with the full weight of the carousel. When you turn the crank, the carousel goes round.

# BLOOMING LOVELY

## Coffee filter flowers

Coffee filters – one per flower
Drink straws
Colours – food colouring or felt-tip pens
Jar or glass, scissors

Cut off the crinkled edge of a coffee filter. Save it for later.

Fold the filter in half, and then again, to form the shape shown, then cut a petal shape with the scissors.

Open out the petals and paint some rough marks on them, about where shown. Allow to dry.

Concertina the petals and crush the middle really tightly, with one end of the crinkled edge in the centre. It all needs to be tight enough to squeeze into the end of a straw, with the crinkled edge directed down through the straw.

When the straw is placed in water, the crinkled edge inside it must be well under the surface.

The water creeps up and along the petals, dragging and separating the colours with it to form beautiful bright flowers.

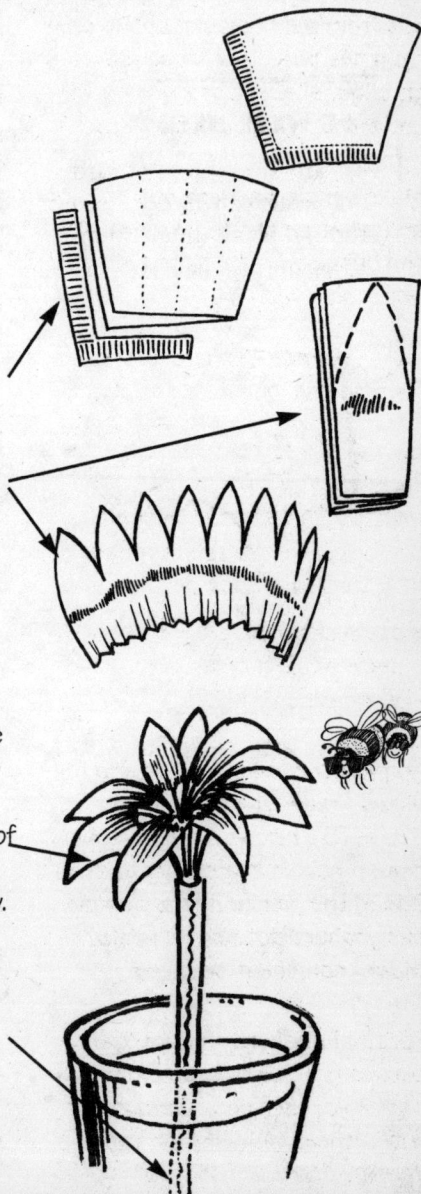

# FRISKY FROGS

**A quick and simple folded frog, and a quick and simple game to enjoy with him.**

## YOU WILL NEED

Postcard-sized piece of card
— a postcard will do,
though blank thin card of
the same size is best.

**1** Fold one of the short sides
down to the long side. Unfold.

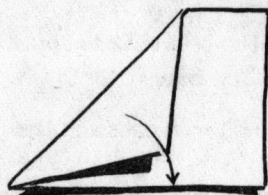

**2** Do the same with the
other short side. You now have
an X-shaped crease on the card.

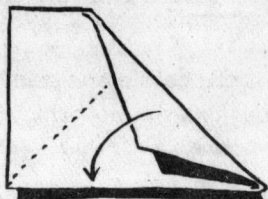

**3** Fold straight across,
backwards, through the centre of
the X.

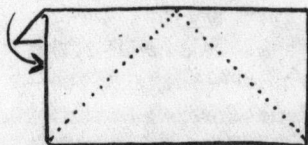

**4** Turn over and fold the top
corners down to the middle of
the bottom edge, to give a
triangle.

**5** Fold the bottom corners
to the top, to give a square.

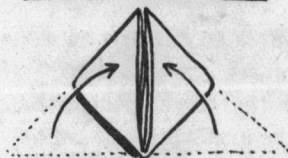

**6** Fold the outside corners in to the centre.

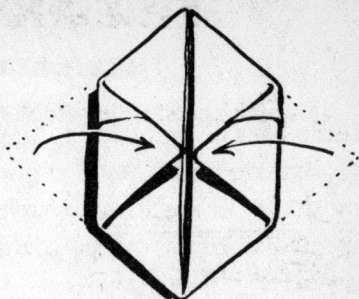

**7** Fold the bottom to the top. You should have an open-envelope sort of shape.

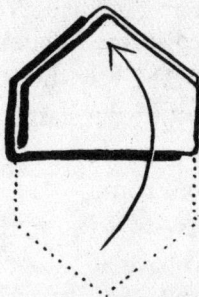

**8** Fold the top triangle on this side down to the the bottom. This is the base of the frog.

**9** Open out and fold out the two triangles you find to form the legs.

**10** Decorate as you like.

Make some more and have a competition to see who can hop their frog into a bowl first. To make your frog hop, press and flick the back.

# STRANGE BUT TRUE

## THE STORY OF ASTRONOMY

People have always tried to find a purpose behind all those stars that twinkle in the sky at night. The ancient Greeks thought they saw shapes in the stars – shapes of people and animals – and they invented stories about gods and monsters to explain how they got there.

When they studied the sky more closely, they began to see patterns in the way the stars moved across the sky from night to night. Most of the stars moved in a regular fashion, but some – the planets – seemed to have a life of their own, moving this way and that seemingly at random. People thought these erratic movements were messages sent to signal important events on Earth, as were comets, meteors and eclipses. Astrologers did a lot of business interpreting the signals and arguing about what they meant.

One thing *nobody* argued about was that the Earth was the centre of the Universe, and everything else moved around it. But in 1500 an obscure monk in Poland, Copernicus, set the world in turmoil. Copernicus was a bit of a wiz at maths. He looked through the figures and reckoned it would all make a lot more sense if we assumed that the centre of the Universe was actually the Sun, and the Earth revolved round it with the other planets.

This was a mixed blessing. On the one hand it neatly explained the erratic behaviour of the planets, and made the Universe a more orderly place. On the other hand it meant that the Earth was no longer the centre of things, but just one planet among many, spinning around on the edge of the cosmos.

This was a tough idea for people to swallow, particularly for the church leaders. For if God had made everything especially for us, as the Bible said, surely He would have put us in the middle. Was Copernicus trying to say the Bible was wrong? Impossible! The church leaders attacked Copernicus, and anyone who supported him.

100 years later the great Italian scientist Galileo turned his newly-invented telescope up to the heavens and made hundreds of new discoveries that proved Copernicus was right. The Church was even more horrid to Galileo, putting him in prison until he stated publicly that the Universe moved around the Earth, which was fixed in the centre. As he left the courtroom he was heard to mutter, "And yet it *does* move."

Sir Isaac Newton put the cap on it with his study of gravity. He realised that gravity not only attracted everything to the Earth, but also kept the planets spinning around the Sun in a predictable way. It even explained eclipses, comets and meteors. A lot of astrologers went out of business.

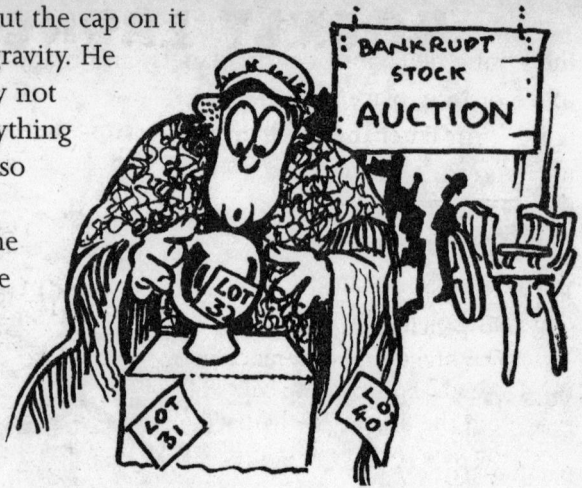

"HOW COME I NEVER FORESAW THIS..."

The Church felt very uncomfortable. By now it was clearly a daft idea to continue insisting the Earth was the centre of the Universe, but they were still bitter about it all, particularly Galileo. In fact the Pope only forgave Galileo officially a couple of years ago!

Since Newton's day there have been hundreds of amazing discoveries out in space – black holes, quasars, super novae, the list is still growing – but if you want to send a rocket to Mars you still reach for Newton's study of gravity to see how to do it.

NEWTON STUDIES THE STARS AND PLANETS

# ROCKET LAUNCHER

**Enter the space race using super ball ballistics.**

Superball
Old pencil stub
(The bigger the difference in
   weight between the ball
   and the pencil, the better.)
Goggles

Get a grown-up to drill a small
hole in the superball, just a little
smaller than the tip of your
pencil. When you push the pencil
in, it should be lightly gripped by
the ball.

Put on your goggles.
Drop the "rocket
launcher" on the floor.
The rocket will shoot
up, almost
to the
ceiling.

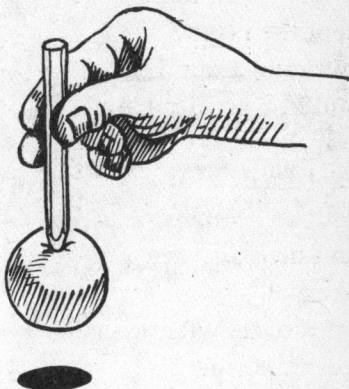

*Warning; Look out! That rocket
really does travel fast.*

As the ball hits the floor it is
travelling at great speed. Its
energy is transferred to the
pencil, which shoots up, leaving
the ball behind. The lighter the
pencil, the higher it flies.

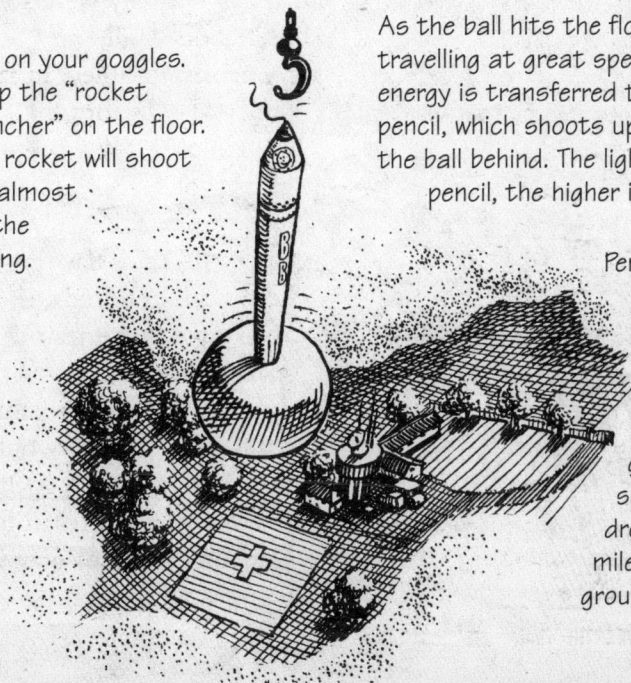

Perhaps one
day real
rockets
will be
launched
from
giant
superballs,
dropped from
miles above
ground!

# BIG BIRD GLIDER

**You can fly through the air with the greatest of ease...
if you find half an hour to make one of these!**

## YOU WILL NEED

Thin card
Scissors
Glue
5 big drinking straws
Paints
4 feathers for decoration
Paper clip
Sticky tape

**1** Fold the card in half.
Unfold. Fold it in thirds. Unfold.

**2** Fold over the top corners
as shown.

**3** Cut off the top corners
and save them for later.

Cut the card in half along the
centre fold. Turn the two halves
through 90 degrees and glue
them together.

**4** Glue a straw in the fold of
the wing to add strength. Fold
the flaps over and glue down.

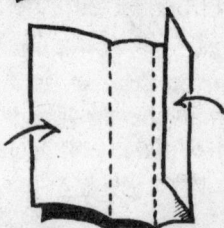

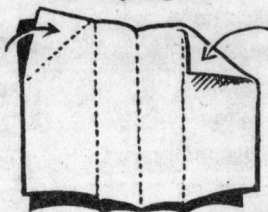

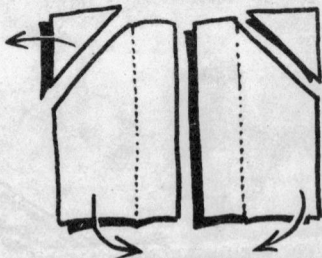

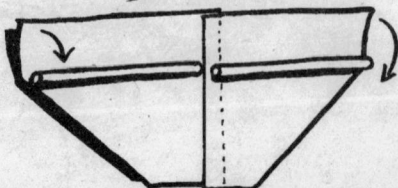

**5** Trim off the corners.

**6** Insert feathers in the back edge of the wing.

Tape three straws to the front of the wing, and fix the other ends between the card triangles you saved from earlier.

**7** Glue the triangles together and fold the sides up to make the bird's head.

Decorate the bird by drawing eyes and painting plumage.

**8** Add one or more paperclips to the beak as needed to balance it, and your glider is ready to fly

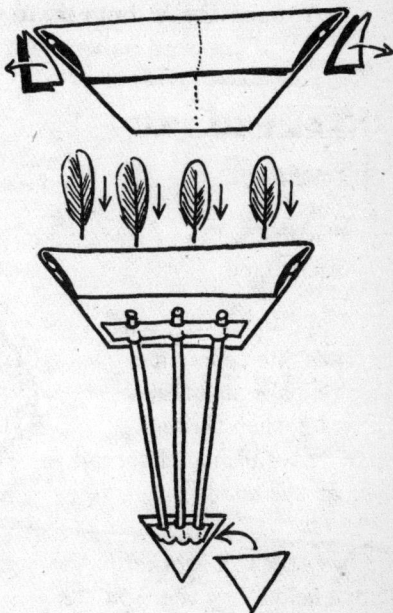

# TETRA BOX KITES

**Spectacular, but easy to make and stunning to fly.**

To make one tetra-kite section take six straws. Thread cotton through each. Leave plenty of thread over at the ends.

Tie five straws together in the shape below. Lay them on the plastic and cut it out as in the drawing. Tape it quite loosely round the shape.

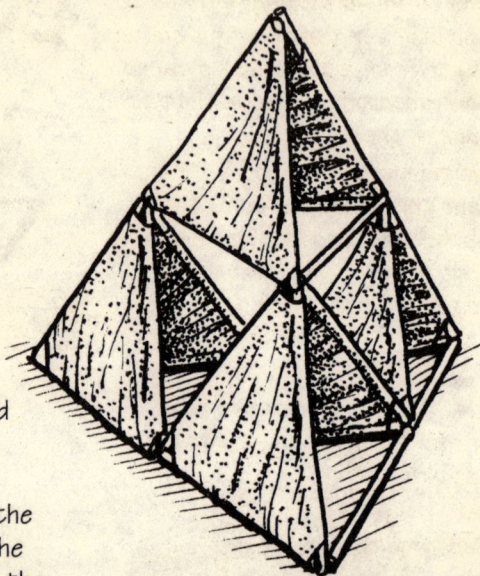

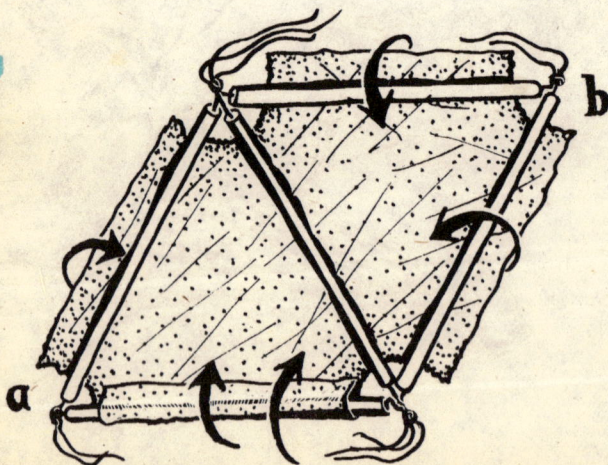

Take one more straw. Attach one end to the left corner (a) and the other end to the right corner (b) to form a triangular pyramid (tetrahedron), as below right.

Do this four times, then tie the four units together at the corners to form the kite shown

left. If you want a giant kite, make four of these, and tie them together the same way.

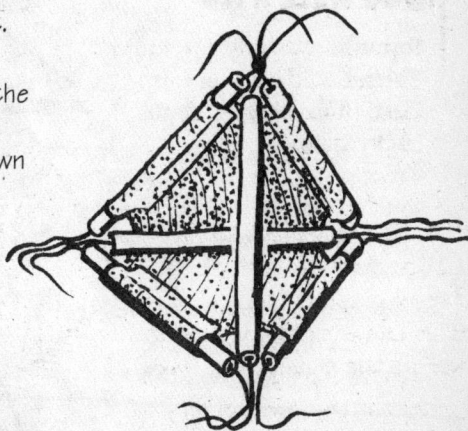

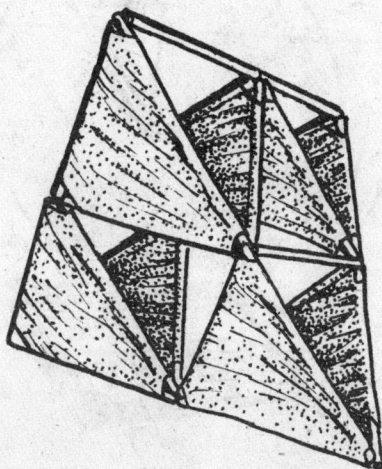

To fly, attach kite string to top corner. Launch with LH corner at bottom.

# HOVER WITH NO BOTHER

**An easy to build hovercraft**

## YOU WILL NEED

Top off a washing-up liquid
  bottle, without the cap
Piece of cardboard, about
  12-15 cm square
Balloon
Glue – cool-melt glue is
  best, but PVA will do

Make a hole in the centre of the
card by sticking a sharp pencil
through from below. Bend the
corners of the card up very
slightly.

Stick the plastic top of the
washing-up liquid bottle over
the hole. Use plenty of glue;
the joint must be airtight.

Hint: if you're using PVA glue,
you'll need a rough surface on
the plastic so the glue can "key"
into it; so rub the plastic with
sand paper or a file.

Once the glue is dry, inflate the
balloon and put it over the top.
(Hold the bottom of the balloon
pinched shut to stop the air
escaping as you do this.)

Put the hovercraft on a flat
surface and let go.

Your hovercraft is kept off the
table by a cushion of air coming
from the balloon. Hovercraft can
glide easily over any flat surface,
water or land. Because they
don't actually touch the ground,
they are virtually friction-free.

# USEFUL BASIC SHAPES

## TO MAKE A SQUARE

Most paper is A4 size.

Fold the short side down to the long side.

Fold the remaining oblong up across the triangle.

Rub the fold really hard – better still, run the tip of your tongue along the crease. Now you can tear the bottom strip off easily, leaving a square.

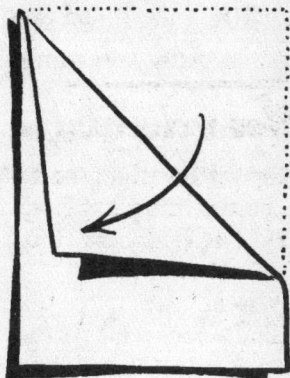

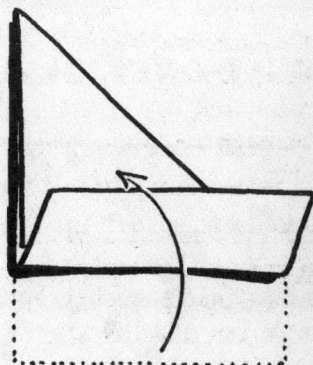

## TO FIND THE CENTRE OF A CIRCLE

Take a piece of paper and place one corner on the edge of the circle.

Mark where the two sides cross the circle. The line joining those points is the diameter. Do it twice, and where the two diameters cross is the centre. This is true however you place the piece of paper!

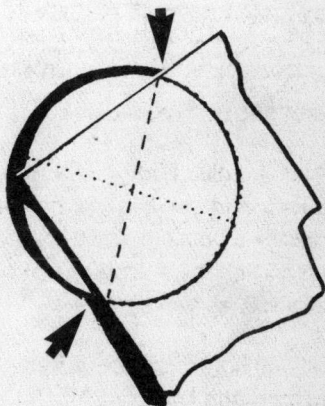

# NOTES ON GLUES

**PVA GLUE** A good all-round glue, though quite slow to dry. It's best for sticking soft things and paper.

**COOL-MELT GLUE** Good where you need bulk, because it's quite thick and strong. It does need a special glue gun for you to use it.

**WAXY GLUES** (eg Pritt) Not strong, but good for paper.

**BLU-TAC** Mostly used for sealing and weighing things down.

## ADULT-ONLY GLUES

**HOT GLUE** Is really hot, but very quick. Will bind, rather than stick, most things. Good for bulk. It is very hot so it must only be used by a grown-up.

**OTHER GLUES** such as epoxy resins are useful because they're strong, but they can also be dangerous, so should only be used with a grown-up to help you.

**NOTE** Smooth surfaces will often stick better if given a rough surface, by rubbing with sandpaper, so that the glue can "key" into it.